Presented to

the Wilson School Library

by

Jeffrey Hartman
~ class of 99 ~

December 1996

THANK YOU VERY MUCH!

© DEMCO, INC.—Archive Safe

Bats
Night Fliers

By BETSY MAESTRO
Illustrated by GIULIO MAESTRO

SCHOLASTIC
HARDCOVER

SCHOLASTIC INC.

New York

Library of Congress Cataloging-in-Publication Data

Maestro, Betsy.
Bats / written by Betsy Maestro; illustrated by Giulio Maestro.
p.   cm.
Summary: Describes the varieties, habitats, behavior, and physical
characteristics of bats.
ISBN 0-590-46150-8
1. Bats — Juvenile literature.   [1. Bats.]   I. Maestro, Giulio, ill.
II. Title.
QL737.C5M34   1994
599.4 — dc20   93-26153
                                                  CIP
                                                  AC

12 11 10 9 8 7 6 5 4   6 7 8 9/9
Printed in the U.S.A.   37

First Scholastic printing, November 1994

The artist used pencils and watercolors
for the illustrations in this book.

Title page illustration: Pallid Bat

Bats are creatures of the night. Long ago, people were afraid of the dark and they thought of bats as mysterious and evil. Because they didn't understand bats, people invented frightening tales of the harm that bats could bring. These stories are sometimes still believed, but most are untrue. Bats are really not scary or harmful at all. The truth about bats will amaze you.

Bats have lived on Earth for about 50 million years. Today, there are nearly 1,000 different kinds of bats in the world. Bats prefer warm climates and large numbers of them live in the tropics. They do not live in the coldest regions of the earth.

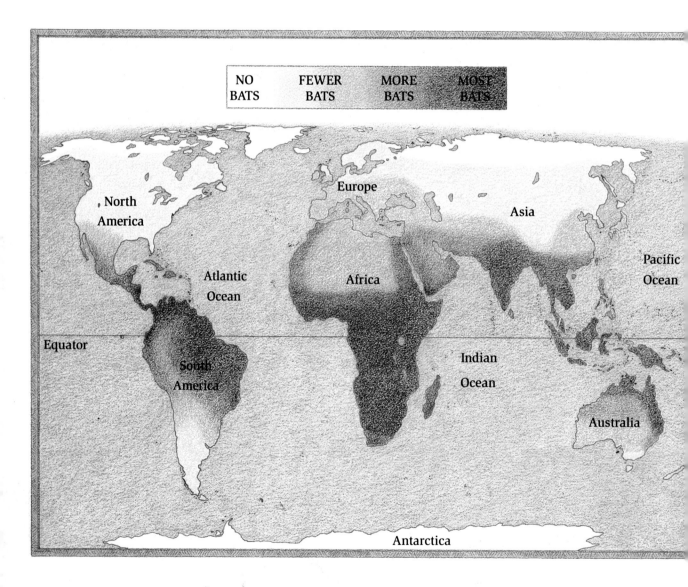

Townsend's Big-eared Bat

People sometimes think bats are related to birds because they both can fly. But bats are not birds. They are mammals like cats, dogs, monkeys, and humans. Mammals have fur- or hair-covered bodies, and usually give birth to live young instead of laying eggs. The females produce milk to feed their babies.

Pallid Bat

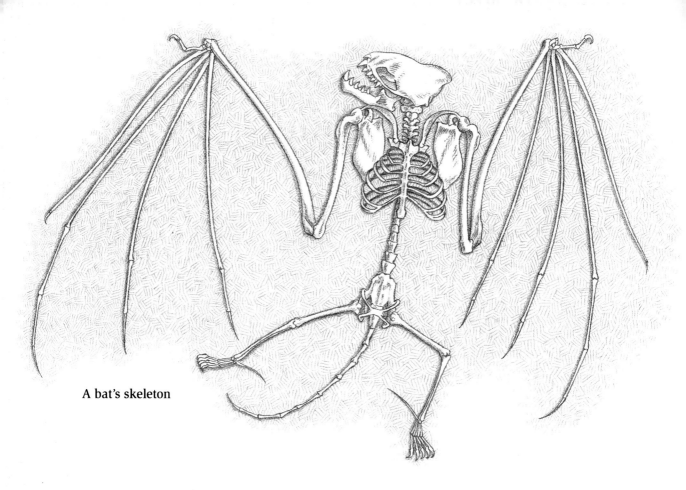

A bat's skeleton

In most ways, bats are similar to other mammals. But in one way, they are very different. Bats can fly — they are the only mammals with wings. A bat's wings are made of two thin layers of strong skin. The skin is stretched tightly and supported by long, bony fingers. A bat actually flies with its hands.

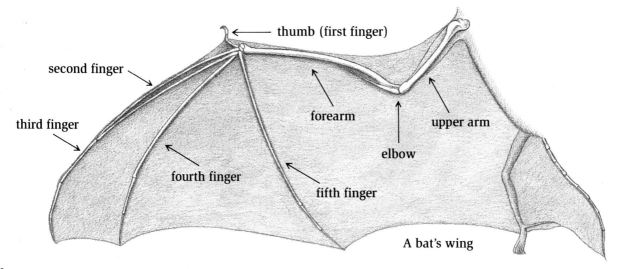

thumb (first finger)

second finger

third finger

forearm

upper arm

elbow

fourth finger

fifth finger

A bat's wing

Bats have four very long fingers and a short, hooklike thumb. The wings are attached to the fingers and often to the legs and tails as well. Bats are excellent fliers. Their wings are very large compared to the size of their bodies. Strong shoulder muscles help to move the wings.

Spotted Bat

Bats are *nocturnal*, or most active at night. They fly in darkness to search for food. During the day, they sleep and rest in their roosts, which may be in caves, trees, buildings, or old animal burrows. Bats sleep upside down, hanging by their toe claws. They often blanket themselves with their wings for protection. When their wings are closed, thousands of tiny wrinkles allow them to fold tightly.

Yellow-winged Bat

Little Brown Bat

A Flying Fox cleans itself with its tongue.

People often think bats are dirty. Actually, they are extremely clean. Like cats, bats use their tongues to clean themselves every day. People also think bats are blind. This is far from true — bats can see perfectly well. Scientists have also found that bats have excellent hearing and a keen sense of smell.

Bats are not all the same size. The bumblebee bats of Thailand are tiny. They are about the size of large bees and weigh less than an ounce. Their wingspan is only about 5 inches. Tropical flying foxes are the world's biggest bats. They can be 16 inches long and weigh as much as 2 pounds. Their open wings often spread 6 feet across.

Giant Flying Fox

Hog-nosed Bat (bumblebee bat)

Bats don't all look alike. Some have brown or gray fur while others have fur that is red or yellowish in color. Some bats are black and white, and a few kinds have bright colors and patterns. Bats can have very large eyes or ears that seem too big for them. Some bats have attractive and appealing faces. Others have strange and unusual features.

Red Bat

Sword-nosed Bat

Butterfly Bat

Epauletted Fruit Bat

Horseshoe Bat

Vampire Bat

Ghost Bat

Leaf-nosed Bat

Black Flying Fox

The bats of the world are divided into two main groups. The large *megabats* and the small *microbats* are very different from one another. The megabats live in the tropical areas of Africa, Asia, and Australia. They are called flying foxes because of their foxlike faces.

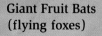

Giant Fruit Bats
(flying foxes)

Epauletted Fruit Bat

These tailless bats have large eyes and very keen vision. They rely on both their vision and excellent sense of smell to find ripe mangoes, bananas, figs, berries, and guava. Megabats chew the fruit with their teeth, swallowing the juice but spitting out the seeds and some of the chewy pulp.

Some megabats drink the nectar of flowers with their extra-long tongues. Others eat pollen, a powder made by flowers. As megabats fly, they drop seeds in new places, helping new plants to grow.

Because they live in warm climates, megabats are active all year. They are friendly, social animals and live in large, noisy colonies. Megabats roost in trees, out in the open, and their loud chattering can be heard from far away.

Megabats often roost in groups called camps.

Woolly False Vampire Bat

Pallid Bat

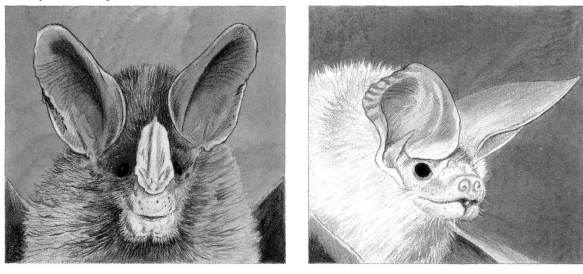

Most of the bats in the world are microbats. They are smaller than the megabats and make their homes almost everywhere on Earth. Over 800 kinds of microbats live in both hot and cold climates. Many of these bats have unusual facial features. Their strange wrinkles, flaps, bumps, and big ears help them find food.

Funnel-eared Bat

Big-eared Bat

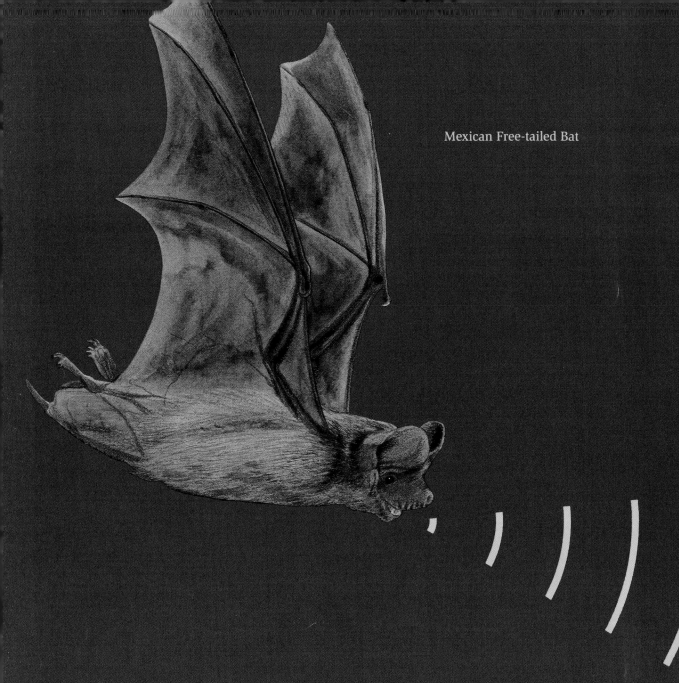

Mexican Free-tailed Bat

Microbats can find food in total darkness without bumping into walls or trees. They *echolocate* or locate objects by listening to echoes. Echolocation works like the radar or sonar in planes or ships. But the microbats' natural system is superior to imitations made by humans.

Using their mouths or noses, microbats can send out hundreds of tiny, high-pitched sounds every second they are in flight. Their facial wrinkles and bumps help to direct these sounds, which cannot be heard by humans. The bats' signals bounce off nearby objects and send back echoes. Bats "read" these echoes to learn what is around them. A tree branch sends back a different echo from a mosquito. Microbats' large ears help them to catch the returning echoes.

Greater Bulldog Bat (fishing bat)

Microbats use echolocation to find food. Some eat tiny insects like gnats and mosquitoes. Other microbats eat fish, swooping low to pluck them out of the water with sharp claws. A few kinds of microbats eat only frogs. Attracted by the frogs' calls, they can tell the difference between the sounds of edible frogs and those of poisonous ones.

Fringe-lipped Bat

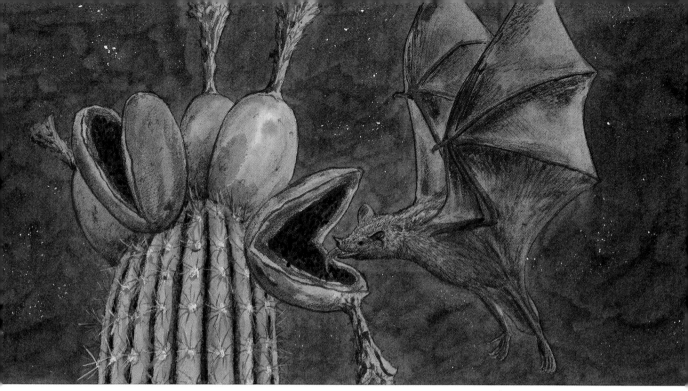

Lesser Long-nosed Bat

Microbats have a varied diet that also includes small animals like mice and birds. In warmer areas, some microbats eat fruit and nectar.

One kind of microbat has a most unusual diet. Vampire Bats live in Mexico and Central America and feed on the blood of cattle and birds. The sleeping animals are often unaware that they have provided a meal for a bat.

Vampire Bats often hop on the ground.

Ghost Bats roost
under leaves.

Some microbats live in huge colonies of thousands, and sometimes
even millions, of bats. Others are solitary and live alone. Microbats
roost in caves, forests, mines, tunnels; under bridges; and in the
attics or eaves of buildings. Very small tropical microbats can roost
inside flowers, in leaf-tents, and in tubelike stalks of bamboo.
In warm or hot climates, bats may use the same roosts all year.

In colder climates, when winter approaches, microbats must either hibernate or fly to warmer areas where they can find food. When bats hibernate, they become totally inactive — their breathing slows and their heart rates and body temperatures drop. While hibernating, they need very little energy from stored fat to stay alive. But if they are disturbed, the bats use their energy too quickly and often die.

Little Brown Bats hibernate in a cave.

Microbats that don't hibernate migrate to warmer places. While some travel only a short distance, others may fly over 800 miles to reach their winter roosts. If they fly with the wind, they can reach speeds of up to 60 miles per hour.

When winter ends, migrating bats return to their summer homes, and the hibernating bats awake. The weather becomes warmer, the insects are plentiful, and the microbats begin their nightly search for food, once again.

Mexican Free-tailed Bats

In warmer climates, microbats may give birth twice during the year, but in most cooler places, babies are born in late spring or early summer. Many microbats that are expecting babies gather together in caves, and form large nursery colonies. At birth, the mother bats hang head up, and catch the babies in pouches formed by their wings and tails.

Most bats give birth to just one baby at a time. The tiny pup, furless at birth, depends totally on its mother, who cleans it and feeds it warm milk. The pup clings tightly to its mother with its teeth and claws. If the baby bat loses its grip, it may fall and be killed.

A mother Little Brown Bat nurses her baby.

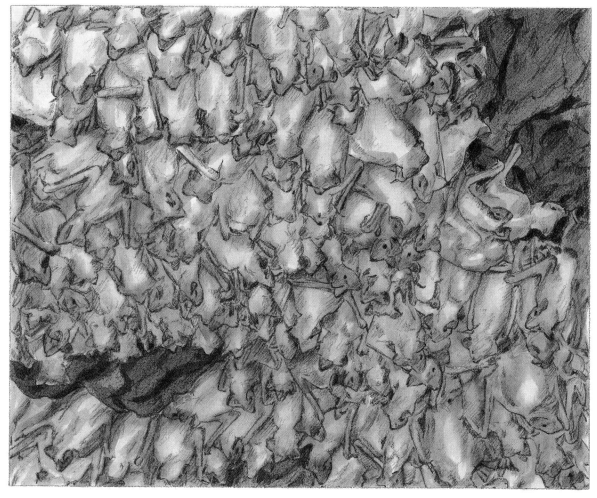

At night, mothers may carry their pups as they search for food. Later, when the babies become too heavy, they will be left behind. The thousands of pups cling to the cave roof and keep each other warm. When the mother bats return, they find and feed their own young. Each mother recognizes the familiar scent and cry of her pup. About a month after birth, baby bats are able to fly by themselves and find their own food.

Mexican Free-tailed Bats

No one knows exactly how many bats there are on Earth. But we do know that Earth would not be the same without bats. A large colony of bats can consume 6,000 tons of insects in a year. A single bat can eat as many as 600 mosquitoes in an hour. Without bats, night-flying insects would rapidly multiply.

Tropical bats are like the bees of the night. They are the only pollinators of some night-opening flowers. And in the rain forests, where too much timber is being cut, seed dispersal aids in new tree growth. In these areas, over 300 kinds of trees and plants depend on fruit-eating bats for their survival.

Mexican Long-nosed Bat

Bats can live for 25 to 30 years. But many are eaten by natural enemies like owls, snakes, raccoons, and hawks. Spring floods can wash out caves and destroy whole colonies of bats. But the most harmful enemies of bats are human beings. Sadly, many bats are killed by humans, accidentally or on purpose.

Jamaican Flower Bat

  The use of insecticides and poisons in the environment can also
cause the death of many bats. Farmers kill bats for eating their fruit.
However, bats only eat fruit that is too ripe to be sold. Cave explorers
and vandals often disturb or destroy hibernating bats, resulting in
the death of thousands of bats.

Some people believe bats attack and bite humans. They also mistakenly think all bats carry the disease *rabies*. But bats are very gentle creatures that rarely bite except when caught and frightened. They don't carry rabies any more often than other mammals. Bats are helpful, not harmful.

People build special houses to attract bats to their neighborhoods.

Bats fly inside the house from the open bottom.

Many bats can cling to the walls inside a bat house.

By protecting bats, people also help themselves. The Chinese have always believed that bats bring good luck. And they probably do. Places where bats live are usually healthy places where all life exists together in the right balance. Humans must learn to be kind to bats. They are nature's helpers and true friends of the earth.

Even in the city, people watch bats on their nightly search for insects.

DID YOU KNOW THAT . . .

Tent-building bats make their own shelter by biting a palm leaf with their teeth. The folded sides form a tent (see Ghost Bats, page 20).

Guano, or bat droppings, is used for fertilizer in many places. The guano is collected from cave floors.

Bats sleep for long periods each day. This rest allows them to live longer than other small mammals.

There are Naked Bats with no fur.

The scientific name for bats is *Chiroptera*, which means hand-wing.

A colony of bats can have as many as 20 million members.

Most bats are small enough to fit in a human hand.

Female Vampire Bats help each other care for their young. Mothers will adopt and care for orphaned Vampire babies.

Red Bats, common in the United States, roost in trees. They hang on with just one foot and look like dead leaves.

Bats that eat nectar may have tongues almost as long as their bodies.

Texas has more bats than any other state. The millions of bats that live in Bracken Cave in Texas can eat a quarter of a million pounds of insects in one night.

Many bats, including Vampire Bats, can be tamed and trained in captivity.

Most bats are very intelligent.

In the Chinese symbol WU-FU, five bats circle the Tree of Life. The bats represent health, wealth, long life, good luck, and happiness. WU-FU is the symbol for Bat Conservation International in Austin, Texas. This organization helps inform people worldwide about the importance of bats.